*Congressional Research Service*

# Salaries of Members of Congress: Congressional Votes, 1990-2013

Ida A. Brudnick
Specialist on the Congress

November 4, 2013

Congressional Research Service

7-5700

www.crs.gov

97-615

# Summary

The U.S. Constitution, in Article I, Section 6, authorizes compensation for Members of Congress "ascertained by law, and paid out of the Treasury of the United States." Throughout American history, Congress has relied on three different methods in adjusting salaries for Members. Specific legislation was last used to provide increases in 1990 and 1991. It was the only method used by Congress for many years.

The second method, under which annual adjustments took effect automatically unless disapproved by Congress, was established in 1975. From 1975 to 1989, these annual adjustments were based on the rate of annual comparability increases given to the General Schedule federal employees. This method was changed by the 1989 Ethics Act to require that the annual adjustment be determined by a formula based on certain elements of the Employment Cost Index (ECI). Under this revised process, annual adjustments were accepted 13 times (scheduled for January 1991, 1992, 1993, 1998, 2000, 2001, 2002, 2003, 2004, 2005, 2006, 2008, and 2009) and denied eleven times (scheduled for January 1994, 1995, 1996, 1997, 1999, 2007, 2010, 2011, 2012, 2013, and 2014). In the 113th Congress, bills have been introduced to alter the adjustment procedure, reduce the pay of Members of Congress, extend the current pay freeze, prohibit pay during a government shutdown, and apply any sequester to Member pay.

Since January, 2009, the salary for Members of Congress has been $174,000. Subsequent adjustments were denied by P.L. 111-8 (enacted March 11, 2009), P.L. 111-165 (May 14, 2010), P.L. 111-322 (December 22, 2010), P.L. 112-175 (September 28, 2012), P.L. 112-240 (January 2, 2013), and P.L. 113-46 (October 17, 2013).

A third method for adjusting Member pay is congressional action pursuant to recommendations from the President, based on the recommendations of the Citizens' Commission on Public Service and Compensation established in the 1989 Ethics Reform Act. Although the Citizens' Commission should have convened in 1993, it did not and has not met since then.

For historical tables on the rate of pay for Members of Congress since 1789; the adjustments projected by the Ethics Reform Act as compared with actual adjustments in Member pay; details on enacted legislation with language prohibiting the automatic annual pay adjustment; and Member pay in constant and current dollars since 1992, see CRS Report 97-1011, *Salaries of Members of Congress: Recent Actions and Historical Tables*, by Ida A. Brudnick.

Members of Congress only receive salaries during the terms for which they are elected. Former Members of Congress may be eligible for retirement benefits. For additional information on retirement benefit requirements, contributions, and formulas, see CRS Report RL30631, *Retirement Benefits for Members of Congress*, by Katelin P. Isaacs.

# Contents

# Contacts

# Introduction

The automatic annual adjustment for Members of Congress is determined by a formula using a component of the Employment Cost Index (ECI), which measures rate of change in private sector pay.[1] The adjustment automatically takes effect unless (1) Congress statutorily prohibits the adjustment; (2) Congress statutorily revises the adjustment; or (3) the annual base pay adjustment of General Schedule (GS) federal employees is established at a rate less than the scheduled increase for Members, in which case the percentage adjustment for Member pay is automatically lowered to match the percentage adjustment in GS base pay.[2] Members may not receive an annual pay adjustment greater than 5%.

This adjustment formula was established by the Ethics Reform Act of 1989.[3] Votes on the annual adjustments since the implementation of this act are contained in this report.

## Source of Member Pay Appropriations and Relationship to Appropriations Bills

Member salaries are funded in a permanent appropriations account.[4] Although discussion of the Member pay adjustment frequently occurs during consideration of the annual appropriations bill funding the U.S. Treasury—currently the Financial Services and General Government appropriations bill—this bill does not contains funds for the annual pay adjustment for Members. This bill only contains funds for the salaries of those employees on the payrolls of the agencies funded in the bill.

Use of this appropriations bill as a vehicle to prohibit the annual pay adjustments for Members developed by custom. A prohibition on Member pay could be offered to any bill, or be introduced as a separate bill.[5]

## Application of the 27th Amendment to the Annual Adjustments

The 27th Amendment to the Constitution, which was proposed on September 25, 1789, and ratified May 7, 1992, states: "No law, varying the compensation for the services of the Senators and Representatives, shall take effect, until an election of Representatives shall have intervened."[6]

---

[1] For specific dollar amounts and statutory authority for each pay adjustment since 1789, a comparison of projected and actual adjustments since 1992, and salaries in constant dollars, see CRS Report 97-1011, *Salaries of Members of Congress: Recent Actions and Historical Tables*, by Ida A. Brudnick. For retirement benefits information, see CRS Report RL30631, *Retirement Benefits for Members of Congress*, by Katelin P. Isaacs.

[2] P.L. 103-356, 108 Stat. 3410, October 13, 1994.

[3] §704(a)(2)(B) of P.L. 101-194, 103 Stat. 1769, November 30, 1989.

[4] P.L. 97-51; 95 Stat. 966; September 11, 1981. See also, for example: "Table 33-1. Federal Programs By Agency and Account" in *Analytical Perspectives, Budget of the United States Government, Fiscal Year 2012* (Washington, GPO: 2011), pp. 2, 3.

[5] For a list of the laws that have previously prohibited Member pay adjustments, see "Table 3. Legislative Vehicles Used for Pay Prohibitions, Enacted Dates, and Pay Language" in CRS Report 97-1011, *Salaries of Members of Congress: Recent Actions and Historical Tables*, by Ida A. Brudnick.

[6] U.S. Constitution, amend. 27.

---

Under the process established by the Ethics Reform Act of 1989, Member pay is automatically adjusted pursuant to a formula. Following ratification of the Amendment, this procedure was challenged in federal court. The reviewing court held that the 27th Amendment does not apply to the automatic annual adjustments,[7] since Congress is considered to already have voted on future adjustments when the automatic mechanism was established. Therefore, according to the court, any adjustment pursuant to the Ethics Reform Act of 1989 is considered a ministerial act and not a separate legislative enactment subject to the 27th Amendment.

Since these decisions, numerous bills have been introduced to change the pay adjustment procedure to require congressional action to effect the pay change. The effect of the 27th Amendment on pay adjustments that may occur separate from the procedures established by the Ethics Reform Act—including, but not limited to, pay reductions, alternative pay adjustment mechanisms, and Article III standing to challenge any future adjustments in federal court[8]— remains unclear.

# Most Recent Developments

## 113th Congress Legislation

As in previous Congresses, bills were introduced in the 113th Congress to

- prohibit adjustments in pay (for example, H.R. 54, H.R. 243, H.R. 636, S. 18, S. 30);[9]

- repeal the automatic pay adjustment provision (for example, H.R. 134, H.R. 150, H.R. 196, S. 65, and H.R. 398);

- change the procedure by which pay for Members of Congress is adjusted or disbursed by linking it to congressional actions or economic indicators, including passage of a budget resolution or reaching the debt limit (for example, H.R. 108, H.R. 167, H.R. 284, H.R. 308, H.R. 310, H.R. 325, H.R. 372, H.R. 397, H.R. 396, H.R. 522, H.R. 593, H.R. 1884, H.R. 2335, H.R. 3234, S. 18, S. 30, and S. 263);

- reduce the pay of Members of Congress (for example, H.R. 37, H.R. 150, H.R. 391, H.R. 396, H.R. 398, and H.R. 1467);

---

[7] See *Boehner v. Anderson*, 809 F.Supp. 138 (D.D.C. 1992) and 30 F.3d 156 (D.C.Cir. 1994).

[8] *Raines v. Byrd*, 521 U.S. 811 (1997).

[9] P.L. 112-240, the American Taxpayer Relief Act of 2012 (January 2, 2013), froze Member pay at the 2009 level for FY2013. Additional, broader, federal pay freeze legislation introduced in the 113th Congress may be potentially related (for example, H.R. 273 and H.R. 933), although under 2 U.S.C. 31(2)(A), Member pay adjustments are "effective at the beginning of the first applicable pay period commencing on or after the first day of the month in which an adjustment takes effect under section 5303 of title 5 in the rates of pay under the General Schedule" and the "first day of the fiscal year in which such adjustment in the rates of pay under the General Schedule takes effect." Pursuant to 5 U.S.C. 5303, General Schedule adjustments are "Effective as of the first day of the first applicable pay period beginning on or after January 1 of each calendar year..." Since 1992, pay adjustments for Members of Congress have been effective (or retroactive to) January 1.

- prohibit pay for Members of Congress during a lapse in appropriations resulting in a government shutdown (for example, H.R. 3160, H.R. 3215, H.R. 3224, H.R. 3234, and H.R. 3236);[10] and

- apply any sequester to Member pay (for example, S. 436, H.R. 1181, H.R. 1478, and H.R. 2677).[11]

## Linking Salaries to Passage of a Concurrent Resolution on the Budget: Votes in the 113th Congress

H.R. 325, which (1) includes language holding congressional salaries in escrow if a concurrent resolution on the budget has not been agreed to by April 15, 2013, and (2) provides for a temporary extension of the debt ceiling through May 18, 2013, was introduced on January 21, 2013.[12] Salaries would be held in escrow for Members in a chamber that has not agreed to a concurrent resolution. Salaries would be released from the escrow account either when that chamber agrees to a concurrent resolution on the budget or the last day of the 113th Congress, whichever is earlier. H.R. 325 was agreed to in the House on January 23, 2013 (285-144, roll call #30), and the Senate on January 31, 2013 (64-34, vote #11). It was enacted on February 4, 2013 (P.L. 113-3).

## Linking Salaries to the Debt Limit: Votes in the 113th Congress

H.R. 807, the Full Faith and Credit Act, was introduced in the House on February 25, 2013. The bill would prioritize certain payments in the event the debt reaches the statutory limit. An

---

[10] Members of Congress continue to receive their pay during a lapse in appropriations for a number of reasons. Article I, § 6 of the Constitution states, "Senators and Representatives shall receive a Compensation for their Services, to be ascertained by Law, and paid out of the Treasury of the United States." The 27th Amendment to the Constitution added: "No law, varying the compensation for the services of the Senators and Representatives, shall take effect, until an election of Representatives shall have intervened." Member salaries have been provided by a permanent, mandatory, appropriation since the enactment of P.L. 97-51 (95 Stat. 966, September 11, 1981, 2 U.S.C. §31 note). Finally, the Government Accountability Office's (GAO) *Principles of Federal Appropriations Law* states: "The salary of a Member of Congress is fixed by statute and therefore cannot be waived without specific statutory authority. B-159835, Apr. 22, 1975; B-123424, Mar. 7, 1975; B-123424, Apr. 15, 1955; A-8427, Mar. 19, 1925; B-206396.2, Nov. 15, 1988 (nondecision letter). However, as each of these cases points out, nothing prevents a Senator or Representative from accepting the salary and then, as several have done, donate part or all of it back to the United States Treasury." (U.S. Government Accountability Office, *Principles of Federal Appropriations Law*, Volume II, Third Edition, Feb. 2006, p. 6-105, http://www.gao.gov/assets/210/202819.pdf).

[11] As in previous years, OMB has determined that Member pay is not subject to sequestration (Appendix A. Preliminary Estimates of Sequestrable and Exempt Budgetary Resources and Reduction in Sequestrable Budgetary Resources by OMB Account - FY 2013 and Appendix B. Preliminary Sequestrable / Exempt Classification by OMB Account and Type of Budgetary Resource, in OMB Report Pursuant to the Sequestration Transparency Act of 2012 (P.L. 112-155), Available at: http://www.whitehouse.gov/sites/default/files/omb/assets/legislative_reports/ stareport.pdf.) Bills have been introduced in prior Congresses that would apply sequestration to Member salaries (for example, H.R. 4675, 99th Cong.; H.Res. 481, 101st Cong.; H.R. 5585, 101st Cong.; S.Amdt. 3044 to S. 3209, 101st Cong.; S.Amdt. 2916 to H.R. 5558, 101st Cong.; S. 3051, 101st Cong.; H.R. 5587, 101st Cong.; H.R. 5718, 101st Cong.; S.Amdt. 2760 to S. 1224, 101st Cong.; S.Amdt. 2881 and S.Amdt. 2884 to S. 110, 101st Cong.; S. 99, 102nd Cong; S. 713, 103rd Cong.; and S.Amdt. 15 to S. 2, 104th Cong.).

[12] The bill states: "If by April 15, 2013, a House of Congress has not agreed to a concurrent resolution on the budget for fiscal year 2014 pursuant to section 301 of the Congressional Budget Act of 1974, during the period described in paragraph (2) the payroll administrator of that House of Congress shall deposit in an escrow account all payments otherwise required to be made during such period for the compensation of Members of Congress who serve in that House of Congress..."

---

amendment, H.Amdt. 61, was offered on May 9, 2013, that would clarify that these obligations would not include compensation for Members of Congress. It was agreed to the same day (340-84, roll call #140). The bill passed the House on May 13, 2013 (221-207, roll call #142).

## January 2014 Member Pay Adjustment Denied

The maximum potential 2014 pay adjustment of 1.2%, or $2,100, was known when the Bureau of Labor Statistics (BLS) released data for the change in the Employment Cost Index (ECI) during the 12-month period from December 2011 to December 2012 on January 31, 2013.[13] The adjustment takes effect automatically each year unless (1) denied statutorily by Congress or (2) limited by the General Schedule (GS) base pay adjustment, since the percentage increase in Member pay is limited by law to the GS base pay percentage increase. The scheduled January 2014 across-the-board increase in the base pay of GS employees under the annual adjustment formula is 1.3%. A scheduled GS annual pay increase may be altered only if the President issues an alternative plan or if a different increase, or freeze, is enacted. The President issued an alternate pay plan for civilian federal employees on August 30, 2013.[14] This plan calls for a January 2014 across-the-board pay increase of 1.0% for federal civilian employees, the same percentage as proposed in the President's FY2014 budget. Legislation has not been enacted to alter the GS adjustment required by the formula.[15] Had the Member pay adjustment not been prohibited by law (P.L. 113-46, enacted October 17, 2013), a GS base pay adjustment of 1.0% would have automatically limited any salary adjustment for Members of Congress to 1.0% ($1,700).

## 112th Congress Legislation[16]

The Senate passed S. 388 on March 1, 2011.[17] The bill would have prohibited Members of the House and Senate from receiving pay, including retroactive pay, for each day that there is a lapse in appropriations or the federal government is unable to make payments or meet obligations because of the public debt limit. The House passed H.R. 1255 on April 1, 2011. The bill would have prohibited the disbursement of pay to Members of the House and Senate during either of these situations.[18] No further action was taken on either bill. On April 8, 2011, the Speaker of the

---

[13] The annual Member pay adjustment was determined by a formula using the Employment Cost Index (private industry wages and salaries, not seasonally adjusted), based on the percentage change reflected in the quarter ending December 31 for the two preceding years, minus 0.5%. The 1.2% adjustment was determined by taking the percentage increase in the index between the quarters ending December 2011 and December 2012, which was 1.7%, and subtracting 0.5%. U.S. Department of Labor, Bureau of Labor Statistics, Employment Cost Index—December 2012 (Washington: January 31, 2013), p. 3. Pursuant to 2 U.S.C. 31(2)(A), this amount is "rounded to the nearest multiple of $100."

[14] Available at http://m.whitehouse.gov/the-press-office/2013/08/30/letter-president-regarding-alternate-pay-civilian-federal-employees.

[15] See, however, language in two House Appropriations Committee reports (H.Rept. 113-90 and H.Rept. 113-91) stating: "The Committee does not include requested funding for a civilian pay increase. Should the President provide a civilian pay raise for fiscal year 2014, it is assumed that the cost of such a pay raise will be absorbed within existing appropriations for fiscal year 2014." (pp. 2-3 and pp. 3-4).

[16] Bills that would affect Member pay have been introduced in the 113th Congress, including H.R. 37, H.R. 54, H.R. 108, H.R. 134, and H.R. 150.

[17] *Cong. Rec.,* March 1, 2011, pp. S1051-1052.

[18] *Cong. Rec.,* April 1, 2011, pp. H2239-2251.

House issued a "Dear Colleague" letter indicating that in the event of a shutdown, Members of Congress would continue to be paid pursuant to the Twenty-Seventh Amendment to the Constitution, which as stated above, states: "No law, varying the compensation for the services of the Senators and Representatives, shall take effect, until an election of Representatives shall have intervened"—although Members could elect to return any compensation to the Treasury.

## January 2013 Member Pay Adjustment Delayed and Then Denied

The maximum potential 2013 pay adjustment of 1.1%, or $1,900, was known when the Bureau of Labor Statistics (BLS) released data for the change in the Employment Cost Index (ECI) during the 12-month period from December 2010 to December 2011 on January 31, 2012.[19] The adjustment takes effect automatically unless (1) denied statutorily by Congress or (2) limited by the General Schedule (GS) base pay adjustment, since the percentage increase in Member pay is limited by law to the GS base pay percentage increase.

The President's budget, submitted on February 13, 2012, proposed an average (i.e., base and locality) 0.5% adjustment for General Schedule (GS) employees.[20] President Obama later stated in a letter to congressional leadership on August 21, 2012, that the current federal pay freeze should extend until FY2013 budget negotiations are finalized.[21] Section 114 of H.J.Res. 117, the Continuing Appropriations Resolution, 2013, which was introduced on September 10, 2012, extended the freeze enacted by P.L. 111-322 through the duration of this continuing resolution. H.J.Res. 117 was passed by the House on September 13 and the Senate on September 22. It was signed by the President on September 28, 2012 (P.L. 112-175). A delay in the implementation of pay adjustments for GS employees automatically delays any scheduled Member pay adjustment.

On December 27, 2012, President Obama issued Executive Order 13635, which listed the rates of pay for various categories of officers and employees that would be effective after the expiration of the freeze extended by P.L. 112-175. The executive order included a 0.5% increase for GS base pay, which automatically lowered the maximum potential Member pay adjustment from 1.1% to 0.5%. As in prior years, schedule 6 of the executive order showed the new rate for Members.[22] The annual adjustments take effect automatically if legislation is not enacted preventing them.

---

[19] The annual Member pay adjustment was determined by a formula using the Employment Cost Index (private industry wages and salaries, not seasonally adjusted), based on the percentage change reflected in the quarter ending December 31 for the two preceding years, minus 0.5%. The 1.1% adjustment was determined by taking the percentage increase in the Index between the quarters ending December 2010 and December 2011, which was 1.6%, and subtracting 0.5%. U.S. Department of Labor, Bureau of Labor Statistics, *Employment Cost Index—December 2011* (Washington: January 31, 2012), p. 3.

[20] Office of Management and Budget, *Analytical Perspectives, Budget of the United States Government, Fiscal Year 2013, Performance and Management* (Washington, GPO: 2012), Table 2-1: Economic Assumptions, p. 17 and p. 114.

[21] "Letter from the President Regarding an Alternative Plan for Pay Increases for Civilian Federal Employees," *Text of a Letter from the President to the Speaker of the House of Representatives and the President of the Senate*, August 21, 2012, available at http://www.whitehouse.gov/the-press-office/2012/08/21/letter-president-regarding-alternative-plan-pay-increases-civilian-feder.

[22] Prior Executive Orders indicating the rates of pay for Members of Congress include: Executive Order 12944 of December 28, 1994; Executive Order 12984 of December 28, 1995; Executive Order 13071 of December 29, 1997; Executive Order 13106 of December 7, 1998; Executive Order 13144 of December 21, 1999; Executive Order 13182 of December 23, 2000; Executive Order 13249 of December 28, 2001; Executive Order 13282 of December 31, 2002; Executive Order 13322 of December 30, 2003; Executive Order 13332 of March 3, 2004; Executive Order 13368 of December 30, 2004; Executive Order 13393 of December 22, 2005; Executive Order 13420 of December 21, 2006; Executive Order 13454 of January 4, 2008; Executive Order 13483 of December 18, 2008; Executive Order 13525 of (continued...)

---

Subsequently, a provision in H.R. 8, the American Taxpayer Relief Act of 2012, which was enacted on January 2, 2013 (P.L. 112-240), froze Member pay at the 2009 level for 2013. The language was included in S.Amdt. 3448, a substitute amendment agreed to by unanimous consent. The bill, as amended, passed the Senate (89-8, vote #251) and the House (257-167, roll call #659) on January 1, 2013.

Additional legislation to prohibit any Member pay adjustment in 2013 was introduced but not enacted in the 112th Congress, including the following:

- Section 5421(b)(1) of H.R. 3630, as introduced in the House, would have prohibited any adjustment for Members of Congress prior to December 31, 2013. Section 706 of the motion to recommit also contained language freezing Member pay.[23] On December 13, 2011, the motion to recommit failed (183-244, roll call #922), and the bill passed the House (234-193, roll call #923). The House-passed version of the bill was titled the "Middle Class Tax Relief and Job Creation Act of 2011." The Senate substitute amendment, which did not address pay adjustments, passed on December 17. It was titled the "Temporary Payroll Tax Cut Continuation Act of 2011." The bill was enacted on February 22, 2012 (P.L. 112-96) without the pay freeze language.

- H.R. 3835, introduced on January 27, 2012, also would have extended the pay freeze for federal employees, including Members of Congress, to December 31, 2013. This bill passed the House on February 1, 2012.

- H.R. 3858, introduced on January 31, 2012, would have extended the pay freeze for Members of Congress. This bill was referred to the Committee on House Administration.

- H.R. 6726, introduced on January 1, 2013, would have extended the pay freeze for federal employees, including Members of Congress, to December 31, 2013. This bill passed the House on January 2, 2013.

- Other bills were introduced in the 112th Congress that included language to freeze Member pay (for example, S. 1931, S. 1936, S. 2065, S. 2079, S. 2210, H.R. 6474, H.R. 6720, H.R. 6721, H.R. 6722).

## January 2011 and January 2012 Member Pay Adjustment Denied

Pay for Members of Congress since January 2009 has been $174,000.

---

(...continued)

December 23, 2009; Executive Order 13561 of December 22, 2010; and Executive Order 13594 of December 19, 2011. Pay rates for Members of Congress generally are listed in "Schedule 6." In most years, the Executive Orders state that the pay rates in this schedule are "effective on the first day of the first applicable pay period beginning on or after January 1." Twice, in 2006 and in 2012, Member pay was statutorily frozen for only a portion of the following year at the time of the issuance of the executive order. In both instances, the executive order listed new pay rates and indicated an effective date following the expiration of the statutory freeze. Pay adjustments in both years were further frozen pursuant to subsequent laws (P.L. 110-5, for the 2007 scheduled pay adjustment, and P.L. 112-240, for the 2013 scheduled pay adjustment). The 2013 freeze was subsequently reflected in Executive Order 13641, which was signed April 5, 2013.

[23] *Congressional Record*, December 13, 2011, p. H8822.

As stated above, projected Member pay adjustments are calculated based on changes in the Employment Cost Index (ECI). The projected 2011 adjustment of 0.9% was known when the Bureau of Labor Statistics (BLS) released data for the ECI change during the 12-month period from December 2008 to December 2009 on January 29, 2010.[24] This adjustment would have equaled a $1,600 increase, resulting in a salary of $175,600.

The 2011 pay adjustment was prohibited by the enactment of H.R. 5146 (P.L. 111-165) on May 14, 2010. H.R. 5146 was introduced in the House on April 27 and was agreed to the same day (Roll no. 226). It was agreed to in the Senate the following day by unanimous consent.

Other bills that would prevent the scheduled 2011 pay adjustment were introduced in both the House and Senate.[25] These include S. 3244, which was introduced in the Senate on April 22, 2010, and agreed to by unanimous consent the same day.[26] The bill was referred to the Committee on House Administration and the House Committee on Oversight and Government Reform.

Additionally, P.L. 111-322, which was enacted on December 22, 2010, prevents any adjustment in GS base pay before December 31, 2012. Since the percent adjustment in Member pay may not exceed the percent adjustment in the base pay of GS employees, Member pay is also frozen during this period. If not limited by GS pay, Members could have received a salary adjustment of 1.3% in January 2012 under the ECI formula.[27]

# Previous Actions and Votes by Year

Below is a chronology of Member pay actions since the implementation of the Ethics Reform Act of 1989, which established the current pay adjustment system. In the section describing each year, the salary for Members and any percent adjustment from the prior year is listed. In general, the salary is followed by a discussion of any action or votes potentially related to the scheduled adjustment that year, as well as any other action related to pay for Members of Congress that occurred during that calendar year.

---

[24] The annual Member pay adjustment was determined by a formula using the Employment Cost Index (private industry wages and salaries, not seasonally adjusted), based on the percentage change reflected in the quarter ending December 31 for the two preceding years, minus 0.5%. The 0.9% adjustment was determined by taking the percentage increase in the Index between the quarters ending December 2008 and December 2009, which was 1.4%, and subtracting 0.5%. U.S. Department of Labor, Bureau of Labor Statistics, *Employment Cost Index—December 2009* (Washington: January 29, 2010), p. 2.

[25] H.R. 4255, introduced December 9, 2009; H.R. 4423, introduced January 12, 2010; S. 3074, introduced March 4, 2010; S. 3198, introduced March 14, 2010; and S. 3244, introduced April 22, 2010.

[26] *Congressional Record*, April 22, 2010, p. S2544.

[27] The annual Member pay adjustment was determined by a formula using the Employment Cost Index (private industry wages and salaries, not seasonally adjusted), based on the percentage change reflected in the quarter ending December 31 for the two preceding years, minus 0.5%. The 1.3% potential adjustment was determined by taking the percentage increase in the index between the quarters ending December 2009 and December 2010, which was 1.8%, and subtracting 0.5%. U.S. Department of Labor, Bureau of Labor Statistics, *Employment Cost Index—December 2010* (Washington: January 28, 2011), p. 3. See also: "Schedule 6—Vice President and Members of Congress," *Adjustments of Certain Rates of Pay*, Executive Order 13594, December 23, 2011, *Federal Register*, vol. 76, no. 247 (Washington, GPO: 2011), pp. 80191-80196.

---

## 2010

Under the formula established in the Ethics Reform Act, Members were originally scheduled to receive a pay adjustment in January 2010 of 2.1%.[28] This adjustment was denied by Congress through a provision included in the FY2009 Omnibus Appropriations Act, which was enacted on March 11, 2009. Section 103 of Division J of the act states, "Notwithstanding any provision of section 601(a)(2) of the Legislative Reorganization Act of 1946 (2 U.S.C. 31(2)), the percentage adjustment scheduled to take effect under any such provision in calendar year 2010 shall not take effect."[29]

Had Congress not passed legislation prohibiting the Member pay adjustment, the 2.1% projected adjustment would have been downwardly revised automatically to 1.5% to match the 2010 GS base pay adjustment.[30]

The provision prohibiting the 2010 Member pay adjustment was added to H.R. 1105 through the adoption of the rule providing for consideration of the bill (H.Res. 184). The rule provided that the provision, which was printed in the report accompanying the resolution,[31] would be considered as adopted. On February 25, 2009, the House voted to order the previous question (393-25, roll call #84) and agreed to the resolution (398-24, roll call #85).[32]

## 2009

Under the formula established in the Ethics Reform Act, Members received a pay adjustment in January 2009 of 2.8%, increasing salaries to $174,000.[33]

As noted above, Member pay adjustments may not exceed the annual base pay adjustment of GS employees.[34] The two pay adjustments may differ because they are based on changes in different quarters of the Employment Cost Index (ECI) or due to actions of Congress and the President. The 2.8% adjustment for Members, however, was less than the projected 2009 base GS

---

[28] The annual Member pay adjustment was determined by a formula using the Employment Cost Index (private industry wages and salaries, not seasonally adjusted), based on the percentage change reflected in the quarter ending December 31 for the two preceding years, minus 0.5%. The 2.1% adjustment was determined by taking the percentage increase in the Index between the quarters ending December 2007 and December 2008, which was 2.6%, and subtracting 0.5%. U.S. Department of Labor, Bureau of Labor Statistics, Employment Cost Index—December 2008 (Washington: January 31, 2009), pp. 2, 17.

[29] P.L. 111-8, March 11, 2009.

[30] The 1.5% GS base adjustment was finalized by U.S. President (Obama), "Adjustments of Certain Rates of Pay," Executive Order 13525, *Federal Register*, vol. 74, December 23, 2009, pp. 69231- 69242.

[31] U.S. Congress, H.Rept. 111-20, *Providing For Consideration Of The Bill (H.R. 1105) Making Omnibus Appropriations For The Fiscal Year Ending September 30, 2009, And For Other Purposes*, 111th Cong., 1st sess., (Washington, GPO: 2009).

[32] *Congressional Record*, February 25, 2009, p. H2655-H2656.

[33] The annual Member pay adjustment was determined by a formula using the Employment Cost Index (private industry wages and salaries, not seasonally adjusted), based on the percentage change reflected in the quarter ending December 31 for the two preceding years, minus 0.5%. The 2.8% adjustment was determined by taking the percentage increase in the Index between the quarters ending December 2006 and December 2007, which was 3.3%, and subtracting 0.5%. U.S. Department of Labor, Bureau of Labor Statistics, Employment Cost Index—December 2007 (Washington: January 31, 2008), pp. 2, 15.

[34] 2 U.S.C. 31(2)(B).

---

adjustment of 2.9%.[35] The GS rate became final on December 18, 2008, when President George W. Bush issued an executive order adjusting rates of pay.[36]

### *Actions to Alter the Automatic Annual Adjustment Procedure*

In March 2009, the Senate considered a number of attempts to alter the automatic annual adjustment procedure for Members of Congress. Senator David Vitter proposed an amendment (S.Amdt. 621) to the FY2009 Omnibus Appropriations Act. The amendment would have repealed the provision of law that provides for the annual adjustments under the Ethics Reform Act. The Senate agreed to a motion to table the amendment on March 10, 2009 (52-45, vote #95). Prior to the vote, the Senate failed to agree to a unanimous consent request to consider S. 542, a bill introduced by Senator Harry Reid which would have eliminated the automatic pay procedure effective February 1, 2011.

On March 17, 2009, the Senate considered S. 620, a bill also introduced by Senator Reid, which would have eliminated the procedure effective December 31, 2010. The Senate agreed to the bill by unanimous consent.[37] The bill was referred to the House Administration Committee and the House Oversight and Government Reform Committee.

The following day, an identical bill, H.R. 1597, was introduced in the House by Representative Jim Matheson. Additional bills that would have affected congressional pay were also introduced in both chambers.[38] Member pay language was also included in Senate amendments intended to be proposed to other bills.[39] No further action was taken.

## 2008

Under the annual pay adjustment procedure, Members originally were scheduled to receive a 2.7% increase in January 2008, based upon the formula set forth in the Ethics Reform Act of 1989.[40] This increase would have raised their salaries to $169,700. The scheduled Member

---

[35] The base pay projection is based upon a number of events. Under the formula established in the Federal Employees Pay Comparability Act (FEPCA, P.L. 101-509, November 5, 1990, 104 Stat. 1429-1431; 5 U.S.C. 5301-5303), the annual across-the-board pay adjustment in January 2009 was projected to equal 2.9%. This percentage, like that adjusting Member pay, was determined based on changes in the Employment Cost Index (ECI), minus 0.5%. It reflects, however, changes from September 2006 to September 2007, rather than December 2006 to December 2007. Additionally, the Consolidated Security, Disaster Assistance, and Continuing Appropriations Act, 2009, enacted on September 30, 2008, provided an overall average (base and locality) pay adjustment of 3.9% for federal civilian employees, including those covered by the General Schedule (P.L. 110-329, Division A, §142(a), September 30, 2008). For additional information on the GS adjustments, see CRS Report RL34463, *Federal White-Collar Pay: FY2009 and FY2010 Salary Adjustments*, by Barbara L. Schwemle.

[36] U.S. President (Bush), "Adjustments of Certain Rates of Pay," Executive Order 13483, *Federal Register*, vol. 73, December 23, 2008, pp. 78587-78598.

[37] "Repealing Automatic Pay Adjustments for Members of Congress," *Congressional Record*, March 17, 2009, S3149.

[38] See, for example, H.R. 156, H.R. 201, H.R. 215, H.R. 282, H.R. 346, H.R. 395, H.R. 566, H.R. 581, H.R. 751, H.R. 1105, H.R. 1597, H.R. 4336, H.R. 4681, H.R. 4720, H.R. 4761, H.R. 4762, S. 102, S. 317, S. 542, S. 1808, S. 3071, S. 3143, and S. 3158. A discharge petition was filed for H.R. 581 on March 23, 2009.

[39] "Text of Amendments," S.Amdt. 3730, an amendment intended to be proposed to S. 3217, *Congressional Record*, April 26, 2010, p. S2663; and, "Text of Amendments," S.Amdt. 3666, an amendment intended to be proposed to H.R. 4872, *Congressional Record*, March 24, 2010, p. S2040.

[40] The annual Member pay adjustment was determined by a formula using the Employment Cost Index (private industry wages and salaries, not seasonally adjusted), based on the percentage change reflected in the quarter ending (continued...)

---

increase was revised to 2.5%, resulting in a salary in 2008 of $169,300, due to factors related to the increase in the base pay of GS employees.

The scheduled January 2008 across-the-board increase in the base pay of GS employees under the annual adjustment formula was 2.5%.[41] A scheduled GS annual pay increase may be altered only if the President issues an alternative plan or if Congress legislates a different increase. President Bush did not issue an alternative plan for the annual pay adjustment, although he issued an alternative plan for the locality pay adjustment on November 27, 2007, providing a 0.5% adjustment (providing an average 3.0% overall adjustment).[42] The Consolidated Appropriations Act, 2008, which was enacted on December 26, 2007, provided a 3.5% average pay adjustment for federal civilian employees. The President issued an executive order allocating this overall percentage between base and locality pay on January 4, 2008.[43] Since the annual base portion of the pay adjustment for GS employees was less than the scheduled Member increase, Member pay was adjusted by the lower rate.

## Actions to Modify or Deny the Scheduled 2008 Member Pay Increase

On June 27, 2007, the House took action potentially relating to the January 2008 Member pay increase. The House agreed (244-181, vote #580) to order the previous question on the rule (H.Res. 517) for consideration of H.R. 2829, the FY2008 Financial Services and General Government Appropriations bill. By ordering the previous question, the House voted to prevent an amendment to the rule from being offered and brought the rule to an immediate vote. The House bill did not contain Member pay language, and the House did not vote on an amendment to accept or reject a Member pay increase.

Under the terms of H.Res. 517, as adopted, an amendment seeking to halt the pay raise was not in order. An amendment to the rule could have waived points of order so as to permit an amendment to the bill prohibiting a pay increase. During floor debate, at least one Member spoke against the previous question and indicated an intention to offer an amendment to the rule to prohibit the increase if it was defeated.[44]

---

(...continued)

December 31 for the two preceding years, minus 0.5%. The 2.7% adjustment was determined by taking the percentage increase in the Index between the quarters ending December 2005 and December 2006, which was 3.2%, and subtracting 0.5%.

[41] The annual GS pay adjustment was determined by a formula using the Employment Cost Index (private industry wages and salaries, not seasonally adjusted), based on the percentage change reflected in the quarter ending September 30 for the two preceding years, minus 0.5%. The 2.5% adjustment was determined by taking the percentage increase in the Index between the quarters ending September 2005 and September 2006, which was 3.0%, and subtracting 0.5%. For additional information, see CRS Report RL33732, *Federal White-Collar Pay: FY2008 Salary Adjustments*, by Barbara L. Schwemle.

[42] U.S. President (Bush), "Text of a Letter from the President to the Speaker of the House of Representatives and the President of the Senate," November 27, 2007. Available at http://www.whitehouse.gov/news/releases/2007/10/20071022-10 html, last visited on January 8, 2008.

[43] U.S. President (Bush), "Adjustments of Certain Rates of Pay," Executive Order 13454, issued January 4, 2008, *Federal Register*, January 8, 2008, vol. 73, pp. 1479-1492.

[44] Consolidated Appropriations Act, 2008 (P.L. 110-161, 121 Stat. 1844, December 26, 2007).

## Vote Summary

- **06/27/07**—The House agreed (244-181, vote #580) to order the previous question on the rule (H.Res. 517) for consideration of H.R. 2829, the FY2008 Financial Services and General Government Appropriations bill. By ordering the previous question, the House voted to prevent an amendment to the rule from being offered, and to bring the rule to an immediate vote. An amendment to the rule could have waived points of order so as to permit an amendment to the bill prohibiting a pay increase. Although H.Res. 517 was an open rule that allowed any germane amendment, an amendment to prohibit the pay adjustment would not have been germane. By agreeing to order the previous question, some Members considered the vote to be against consideration of an amendment prohibiting a pay raise. Had the House not agreed to a motion to order the previous question, they argued, a Member could have offered an amendment to the rule related to the pay adjustment. Under the terms of H.Res. 517, as adopted, an amendment seeking to halt the pay raise was not in order. During floor debate, at least one Member spoke against ordering the previous question and indicated that, if the motion was defeated, he intended to offer an amendment to the rule to prohibit the pay increase.[45]

# 2007

Members did not receive the annual pay adjustment of 1.7% scheduled for January 1, 2007, as a consequence of the votes Congress had taken in both 2006 and 2007. The salary of Members remained at the 2006 level of $165,200.

Members initially had been scheduled to receive a 2.0% annual adjustment in January 2007, increasing their salary to $168,500.[46] This increase was automatically revised downward to 1.7% to match GS base pay. Based on a formula required under the annual comparability pay procedure,[47] General Schedule (GS) employees were authorized to receive a base pay increase of 1.7% in January 2007.[48] The percentage was confirmed when the President issued an alternative plan for the locality pay adjustment, but not base pay, on November 30, 2006, and then an executive order issued on December 21, 2006, authorizing the average 2.2% pay adjustment for General Schedule employees.[49]

---

[45] *Congressional Record*, daily edition, vol. 153, June 27, 2007, pp. HH7278-H7283.

[46] The annual Member pay adjustment was determined by a formula using the Employment Cost Index (private industry wages and salaries, not seasonally adjusted), based on the percentage change reflected in the quarter ending December 31 of the two preceding years, minus 0.5%. The 2.0% adjustment was determined by taking the percentage increase in the Index between the quarters ending December 2004 and December 2005, which was 2.5%, and subtracting 0.5%.

[47] The annual GS pay adjustment was determined by a formula using the Employment Cost Index (private industry wages and salaries, not seasonally adjusted), based on the percentage change reflected in the quarter ending September 30 of the two preceding years, minus 0.5%. The 1.7% adjustment was determined by taking the percentage increase in the Index between the quarters ending September 2004 and September 2005, which was 2.2%, and subtracting 0.5%.

[48] U.S. Department of Labor, Bureau of Labor Statistics, *Employment Cost Index—September 2005* (Washington: October 28, 2005), pp. 2, 14.

[49] U.S. President (Bush), "Text of a Letter from the President to the Speaker of the House of Representatives and the President of the Senate," November 30, 2006; U.S. President (Bush), "Adjustments of Certain Rates of Pay," Executive Order 13420, *Federal Register*, vol. 71, December 26, 2006, pp. 77569-77580.

---

## *Actions Related to the Scheduled Annual Adjustment for 2007*

A series of votes in 2006 and 2007 prevented the scheduled adjustment. The continuing resolution enacted on December 8, 2006 (P.L. 109-383), postponed any increase until February 16, 2007. The Revised Continuing Appropriations Resolution, 2007, which became law on February 15, 2007 (P.L. 110-5), further prevented the scheduled 2007 adjustment from taking effect.

On March 8, 2006, the Senate voted to change the application of the annual comparability adjustment for Members by denying an increase for those Members who voted against receiving one. On June 13, 2006, the House ordered the previous question on the rule for consideration of the FY2007 Treasury appropriations bill. This action prevented amendments to the rule, including those related to Member pay, from being considered.

Congress subsequently voted to delay the scheduled January 2007 pay increase until February 2007. Congressional action, however, blocked any pay increase in 2007. After the relative increases in congressional pay as compared to the federal minimum wage became a campaign issue, Congress delayed any increase until February 16, 2007.

## *Vote Summary*

- **06/13/06**—The House agreed (249-167, vote #261) to order the previous question on the rule (H.Res. 865) for consideration of H.R. 5576, the FY2007 Transportation and Treasury Appropriation bill. By ordering the previous question, the House voted to prevent an amendment to the rule from being offered, and to bring the rule to an immediate vote. An amendment to the rule could have waived points of order so as to permit an amendment to the bill prohibiting a pay increase. Although H.Res. 865 was an open rule that allowed any germane amendment, an amendment to prohibit the pay adjustment would not have been germane. By agreeing to order the previous question, some Members considered the vote to be against consideration of an amendment prohibiting a pay raise. Had the House not agreed to a motion to order the previous question, they argued, a Member could have offered an amendment to the rule related to the pay adjustment. Under the terms of H.Res. 865, as adopted, an amendment seeking to halt the pay raise was not in order. During floor debate, Representative Jim Matheson made known his intention to offer an amendment to the rule to prohibit the increase, and spoke against the previous question so that his amendment could receive a waiver to be considered.[50]

- **12/8/06**—Section 137 of P.L. 109-383 (120 Stat. 2679), which amended the Continuing Appropriations Resolution, delayed any increase in Member pay until February 16, 2007.

- **02/15/07**—The Revised Continuing Appropriations Resolution, 2007, became law (P.L. 110-5, 121 Stat. 12). Section 115 stated that the adjustment in Member pay scheduled for 2007 shall not take effect.

---

[50] *Congressional Record*, daily edition, vol. 152, June 13, 2006, pp. H3820-H3821.

## *Actions to Deny Adjustments or Benefits for Certain Members*

In 2007, both the House and Senate took action on bills that would target the adjustments or benefits of Members under certain circumstances. Neither of these provisions became law.

- **1/18/07**—The Senate passed (96-2, vote #19) S. 1, the Honest Leadership and Open Government Act of 2007. The bill contained a provision (§116) that would deny an annual pay adjustment to Members of Congress who vote for an amendment to prohibit an annual adjustment for Members, or who voted against the tabling of an amendment to prohibit the increase. This language was not included in the House amendment or in the final version of the bill, which became P.L. 110-81.

- **1/23/07**—The House passed (431-0, vote #49) H.R. 476. The bill would have denied pension benefits to Members of Congress if an individual is convicted of committing certain offenses while a Member of Congress. The bill was referred to the Senate Committee on Homeland Security and Governmental Affairs and no further action was taken.

# 2006

Members received a pay adjustment of 1.9% in January 2006, increasing their salary to $165,200 from $162,100.[51]

This increase became official when President Bush issued an executive order on December 22, 2005, containing his allocation of a 3.1% pay increase for GS federal employees, 2.1% for base pay and an average of 1.0% for locality pay.[52] By setting the GS base pay component at a rate (2.1%) greater than the scheduled 1.9% Member pay increase, Members were able to receive the full 1.9% adjustment.

## *Actions Related to the Scheduled Annual Adjustment for 2006*

In 2005, during consideration of the January 2006 adjustment, the House held one vote potentially relating to the pending January 2006 increase, and the Senate voted to deny the adjustment.

The House vote occurred June 28, 2005, when it agreed to a rule providing for consideration of H.R. 3058, the FY2006 Transportation, Treasury, and Housing and Urban Development, the Judiciary, District of Columbia, and Independent Agencies Appropriations bill. Special waiver language was needed in the rule to permit House consideration of an amendment that would prohibit the scheduled January 2006 pay increase. In the absence of such language, a pay amendment was out of order.

---

[51] The annual pay adjustment was determined by a formula using the Employment Cost Index (private industry wages and salaries, not seasonally adjusted), based on the percentage change reflected in the quarter ending December 31 of the two preceding years, minus 0.5%. The 1.9% adjustment was determined by taking the percentage increase in the Index between the quarters ending December 2003 and December 2004, which was 2.4%, and subtracting 0.5%.

[52] The 3.1% GS pay increase had been approved earlier by Congress as a provision in the FY2006 Transportation and Treasury Appropriation Act, signed into P.L. 109-115 on November 30, 2005. Congress did not specify an allocation between base and locality pay in the act, since the President makes that determination.

---

This action was considered by some to be approval of an increase since the vote had the effect of not allowing Members to offer and consider nongermane amendments to the bill. They argued that if nongermane amendments had been allowed, one could have been offered to modify or deny the scheduled 1.9% Member pay increase.

Others, however, expressed interest in introducing other nongermane amendments on unrelated issues. As a consequence, it cannot be said with any degree of certainty that Members would have voted to deny a pay increase if they had been given an opportunity.

The Senate agreed October 18, 2005, to an amendment, by a vote of 92 to 6, to prohibit the scheduled January 2006 Member pay adjustment.[53] The prohibition did not apply to the 1.9% increase scheduled for other top-level federal officials in the executive and judicial branches. The amendment was struck in conference.

## Vote Summary

- **03/08/06**—The Senate agreed (voice vote) to an amendment denying an annual pay adjustment to Members of Congress who vote for an amendment to prohibit an annual adjustment for Members, or who voted against the tabling of an amendment to prohibit the increase. The amendment (S.Amdt. 2934) was offered by Senator James Inhofe during consideration of S. 2349, the 527 Reform bill. The bill was not enacted into law.

- **06/28/05**—The House agreed (263-152, vote #327) to order the previous question on the rule (H.Res. 342) for consideration of H.R. 3058, the FY2006 Transportation and Treasury Appropriation bill. By ordering the previous question, the House voted to prevent an amendment to the rule from being offered, and to bring the rule to an immediate vote. An amendment to the rule could have waived points of order so as to permit an amendment to the bill prohibiting a pay increase. Although H.Res. 342 was an open rule that allowed any germane amendment, an amendment to prohibit the pay adjustment would not have been germane. By agreeing to order the previous question, some Members considered the vote to be against consideration of an amendment to permit a pay raise prohibition to be offered. Had the House not agreed to a motion to order the previous question, they argued, a Member could have offered an amendment to the rule related to the pay adjustment. Under the terms of H.Res. 342, as adopted, an amendment seeking to halt the pay raise was not in order. During floor debate, Representative Jim Matheson made known his intention to offer an amendment to the rule to prohibit the increase, and spoke against the previous question so that his amendment could receive a waiver to be considered.[54]

- **10/18/05**—The Senate agreed (92-6, vote #256) to an amendment prohibiting the 2006 annual federal pay adjustment for Members of Congress only. It did not apply to top-level executive and judicial branch officials. The amendment (S.Amdt. 2062), was offered by Senator Jon Kyl during consideration of H.R.

---

[53] *Congressional Record*, daily edition, vol. 151, no. 132, October 18, 2005, pp. S11458-60.

[54] *Congressional Record*, daily edition, vol. 151, no. 88, June 28, 2005, p. H5279.

3058, FY2006 Transportation and Treasury Appropriation bill. The Senate provision was dropped in conference.

# 2005

Members received a pay adjustment of 2.5% in January 2005, increasing their salary to $162,100 from $158,100.

## *Actions Related to the Scheduled Annual Adjustment for 2005*

One vote potentially relating to the Member pay adjustment scheduled for January 2005 was held in 2004. On September 14, the House agreed to a rule providing for consideration of H.R. 5025, the FY2005 Transportation and Treasury Appropriation bill. Special waiver language was needed in the rule to permit House consideration of an amendment that would prohibit the scheduled January 2005 pay increase. In the absence of such language, a pay amendment was not in order.

This House action, however, was considered by some to be approval of an increase since the vote had the effect of not allowing Members to offer and consider nongermane amendments to the bill. They argued that if nongermane amendments had been allowed, one could have been offered to modify or deny the scheduled 2.2% Member pay increase.

Alternatively, however, a few Members expressed interest in introducing other nongermane amendments on entirely different issues. As a consequence, it cannot be said with any degree of certainty that Members would have voted to deny a pay increase had they had been given an opportunity.

## *Vote Summary*

- **09/14/04**—The House agreed (235-170, vote #451) to order the previous question on a rule (H.Res. 770) providing for consideration of H.R. 5025, the FY2005 Transportation and Treasury Appropriations bill. By ordering the previous question, the House voted to prevent an amendment to the rule from being offered, and to bring the rule to an immediate vote. An amendment to the rule could have waived points of order so as to permit an amendment to the bill prohibiting a pay increase. Although H.Res. 770 was an open rule that allowed any germane amendment, an amendment to prohibit the pay adjustment would not have been germane. By agreeing to order the previous question, some Members considered the vote to be against consideration of an amendment to permit a pay raise prohibition to be offered. Had the House not agreed to a motion to order the previous question, they argued, a Member could have offered an amendment to the rule related to the pay adjustment. Under the terms of H.Res. 770, as adopted, an amendment seeking to halt the pay raise was not in order.

# 2004

Members received a pay adjustment of 2.2% in 2004, increasing their salary to $158,100 from $154,700. The adjustment was effective in two stages. The first adjustment increased Members' salary by 1.5%, to which they were initially limited because by law they may not receive an annual adjustment greater than the increase in the base pay of GS federal employees. After the passage of the FY2004 Consolidated Appropriations Act, which provided an average 4.1% GS pay increase, Members received the full 2.2% pay increase, with 0.7% retroactive to the first pay period in January 2004.[55]

## Actions Related to the Scheduled Annual Adjustment for 2004

Two potentially related votes related to the scheduled January 2004 adjustment. Action taken by the House on vote #463 (240-173) was considered by some to be approval of an annual increase since the vote had the effect of not allowing Members to offer and consider nongermane amendments to the bill. They argued that if nongermane amendments had been allowed, one could have been offered to modify or deny the scheduled 2.2% Member pay increase.

While some Members have characterized this as a vote for the raise, some Members expressed interest in introducing other nongermane amendments on entirely different issues. As a consequence, it cannot be said with any degree of certainty that Members would have voted to deny a pay increase if they had been given an opportunity.

On October 23, 2003, the Senate voted to table an amendment to prohibit the scheduled adjustment.

## Vote Summary

- **09/04/03**—The House agreed (240-173, vote #463) to order the previous question on a rule (H.Res. 351) providing for consideration of H.R. 2989, the FY2004 Transportation and Treasury Appropriations bill. By ordering the previous question, the House voted to prevent an amendment to the rule from being offered, and to bring the rule to an immediate vote. An amendment to the rule could have waived points of order so as to permit an amendment to the bill prohibiting a pay increase. Although H.Res. 351 was an open rule that allowed any germane amendment, an amendment to prohibit the pay adjustment would not have been germane. By agreeing to order the previous question, some Members considered the vote to be against consideration of an amendment to permit a pay raise prohibition to be offered. Had the House not agreed to a motion to order the previous question, they argued, a Member could have offered an amendment to the rule related to the pay adjustment. Under the terms of H.Res. 351, as adopted, an amendment seeking to halt the pay raise was not in order.

- **10/23/03**—The Senate agreed (60-34, vote #406) to a motion to table an amendment offered by Senator Russell Feingold to H.R. 2989, the FY2004 Transportation and Treasury Appropriation bill, to block the pending January 2004 salary increase for Members. The amendment did not apply to other top-level federal officials.

---

[55] P.L. 108-199; January 23, 2004; 118 Stat. 359.

# 2003

Members received a pay adjustment of 3.1% in January 2003, increasing their salary to $154,700 from $150,000.

## *Actions Related to the Scheduled Annual Adjustment for 2003*

Members originally were scheduled to receive a 3.3% adjustment under the formula.[56] By law, however, they were limited to the rate of increase in the base pay of General Schedule (GS) employees (3.1%), also effective in January 2003.

Both houses held votes related to the scheduled January 2003 annual adjustment for Members. On July 18, 2002, the House agreed to a rule providing for consideration of H.R. 5120, the FY2003 Treasury and General Government Appropriations bill. Special waiver language was needed in the rule to permit House consideration of an amendment that would prohibit the scheduled January 2003 pay increase. In the absence of such language, a pay amendment was out of order.

On November 13, 2002, the Senate voted to table an amendment to prohibit the scheduled January 2003 annual adjustment from taking effect for Members of Congress. The amendment was offered to H.R. 5005, the Homeland Security Act of 2002.

## *Vote Summary*

- **07/18/02**—The House agreed (258-156, vote #322) to order the previous question on a rule (H.Res. 488) providing for consideration of H.R. 5120, the FY2003 Treasury Appropriations bill. By ordering the previous question, the House voted to prevent an amendment to the rule from being offered, and to bring the rule to an immediate vote. An amendment to the rule could have waived points of order so as to permit an amendment to the bill prohibiting a pay increase. Although H.Res. 488 was an open rule that allowed any germane amendment, an amendment to prohibit the pay adjustment would not have been germane. By agreeing to order the previous question, Members voted not to consider an amendment to permit a pay raise prohibition amendment to be offered. Had the House not agreed to a motion to order the previous question, a Member could have offered an amendment to the rule related to the pay adjustment. Under the terms of H.Res. 488, as adopted, an amendment seeking to halt the pay raise was not in order. The vote to order the previous question (and not allow any amendment to the rule) was seen by some as a vote to accept a pay adjustment.

- **11/13/02**—The Senate agreed (58-36, vote #242) to a motion to table an amendment offered by Senator Russell Feingold to H.R. 5005, the Homeland

---

[56] The annual pay adjustment was determined by a formula using the Employment Cost Index (private industry wages and salaries, not seasonally adjusted), based on the percentage change reflected in the quarter ending December 31 of the two preceding years, minus 0.5%. The 3.3% adjustment was determined by taking the percentage increase in the Index between the quarters ending December 2000 and December 2001, which was 3.8%, and subtracting 0.5%.

---

Security Act of 2002, to block the pending January 2003 salary increase for Members. The amendment did not apply to other top-level federal officials.

# 2002

Members received a pay adjustment of 3.4% in January 2002, increasing their salary to $150,000 from $145,100.

## Actions Related to the Scheduled Annual Adjustment for 2002

In 2001, the House held one vote potentially related to the scheduled pay adjustment, and the Senate twice considered the germaneness of Member pay adjustment amendments.

The House, on July 25, 2001, agreed to a rule providing for consideration of H.R. 2590, the FY2002 Treasury and General Government Appropriations bill. Special waiver language was needed in the rule to permit House consideration of an amendment that would prohibit the scheduled January 2002 pay increase. In the absence of such language, a pay amendment was out of order.

The Senate presiding officer, on October 24, sustained a point of order against an amendment to the FY2002 foreign operations appropriations bill to block the 2002 increase because the amendment was not germane under Senate Rule 16. On December 7, the Senate sustained (33-65) a point of order that an amendment to prohibit Members from receiving the January 2002 increase was not germane, and the amendment fell. The amendment was offered during Senate consideration of H.R. 3338, the FY2002 Department of Defense appropriation bill.

## Vote Summary

- **07/25/01**—The House agreed (293-129, vote #267) to order the previous question on a rule (H.Res. 206) providing for consideration of H.R. 2590, the FY2002 Treasury, Postal Service, and General Government Appropriations bill. H.Res. 206 was an open rule that allowed any germane amendment; an amendment to prohibit the pay adjustment, however, would not have been germane. By agreeing to order the previous question, Members voted not to consider an amendment to permit a pay raise prohibition amendment to be offered. Had the House not agreed to a motion to order the previous question, a Member could have offered an amendment to the rule related to the pay adjustment. Under the terms of H.Res. 206, an amendment seeking to halt the pay raise was not in order. The vote to order the previous question (and not allow any amendment to the rule) was seen by some as a vote to accept a pay increase.

- **10/24/01**—The Senate sustained a point of order against an amendment, offered by Senators Russell Feingold and Max Baucus, to block the pending January 2002 salary increase. The Senate sustained the point of order because the amendment was not germane under Senate Rule 16. The action was taken during consideration of H.R. 2506, the FY2002 foreign operations, export financing, and related programs appropriations bill.

- **12/07/01**—The Senate rejected (33-65, voted #360) a claim that an amendment offered by Senator Russell Feingold to prohibit Members from receiving the

January 2002 increase was germane, and the chair then sustained a point of order that the amendment authorized legislation on an appropriation bill. The amendment was offered during floor consideration of H.R. 3338, the FY2002 Department of Defense Appropriations bill.

# 2001

Members received a January 2001 annual pay adjustment of 2.7%, which increased their salary to $145,100 from $141,300.

## Actions Related to the Scheduled Annual Adjustment for 2001

Under the Ethics Reform Act, Members originally were scheduled to receive a January 2001 annual pay adjustment of 3.0%. This adjustment automatically was revised downward to 2.7% to match the GS base pay increase.[57]

On July 20, 2000, the House agreed to the rule providing for consideration of H.R. 4871, the FY2001 Treasury and General Government Appropriations bill. Special waiver language was needed in the rule to permit House consideration of an amendment that would prohibit the scheduled January 2001 pay increase. In the absence of such language, a pay amendment was not in order.

On September 9, 2000, the Senate rejected the conference report on H.R. 4516, the FY2001 Legislative Branch Appropriations bill, in part because Senators had not previously had a chance to introduce an amendment prohibiting the scheduled January 2001 pay increase.

## Vote Summary

- **07/20/00**—The House agreed (250-173, vote #419) to order the previous question on a rule (H.Res. 560) providing for consideration of H.R. 4871, the FY2001 Treasury, Postal Service, and General Government Appropriations bill. H.Res. 560 was an open rule that allowed any germane amendment; an amendment to prohibit the pay adjustment, however, would not have been germane. By agreeing to order the previous question, Members voted not to consider an amendment to permit a pay raise prohibition amendment to be offered. Had the House not agreed to a motion to order the previous question, a Member could have offered an amendment to the rule related to the pay adjustment. Under the terms of H.Res. 560, as adopted, an amendment seeking to halt the pay raise was not in order. The vote to order the previous question (and not allow any amendment to the rule) was seen by some as a vote to accept a pay adjustment.

---

[57] The annual pay adjustment was determined by using the Employment Cost Index (private industry wages and salaries, not seasonally adjusted), based on the percentage change reflected in the quarter ending December 31 of the two preceding years, minus 0.5%. The scheduled January 2001 adjustment was originally 3.0%, and was determined by taking the percentage increase in the Index between the quarter ending December 31, 1998, and the quarter ending December 31, 1999, which was 3.5%, and subtracting 0.5%. However, Members were limited by law to the increase in the base pay of GS employees, which was 2.7%.

- **09/20/00**—The Senate rejected (28-69, vote #253) the conference report on H.R. 4516, the FY2001 Legislative Branch Appropriations bill; the conference report also contained the FY2001 Treasury and General Government Appropriations bill. The Treasury bill had not been initially considered and amended on the Senate floor. The conference report was rejected, according to at least one Member, in part because Senators had not had a chance to introduce an amendment to the FY2001 Treasury bill to prohibit the scheduled January 2001 pay raise.[58] Since Members customarily had offered amendments to prohibit scheduled pay increases in the Treasury bill, some Senators felt that they were denied an opportunity to introduce an amendment to block the scheduled January 2001 pay increase. Some Members also stated that they felt that they were denied the opportunity to debate the merits of a raise and conduct a vote.[59] On December 14, 2000, the text of the FY2001 Treasury and General Government Appropriations bill was introduced as H.R. 5658, which was not considered by either house, but incorporated by reference in H.R. 4577, the FY2001 Omnibus Consolidated Appropriations bill (P.L. 106-554).

## 2000

Members received a scheduled January 1, 2000, annual pay adjustment of 3.4%, which increased their salary to $141,300 from $136,700.[60]

### *Actions Related to the Scheduled Annual Adjustment for 2000*

On July 14, 1999, several Members testified before the House Rules Committee seeking approval to offer an amendment to H.R. 2490, the FY2000 Treasury and General Government Appropriations bill, that would block a pay increase for Members, while allowing an increase for other federal employees. On July 15, the House agreed to the rule providing for consideration of H.R. 2490. Special waiver language was needed in the rule to permit House consideration of an amendment that would prohibit the scheduled January 2000 pay increase. In the absence of such language, a pay amendment was not in order.

Although a subsequent appropriations bill, H.R. 3194, provided for a 0.38% across-the-board rescission in discretionary budget authority for FY2000, H.R. 3194 did not contain language reducing the pay of Members of Congress. H.R. 3194, the FY2000 Consolidated Appropriations Act, was signed into law on November 29, 1999 (P.L. 106-113).

---

[58] Sen. Paul Wellstone, remarks in the Senate, *Congressional Record*, daily edition, vol. 146, September 19, 2000, pp. S 8739-S8741.

[59] Ibid.

[60] The annual pay adjustment was determined by using the Employment Cost Index (private industry wages and salaries, not seasonally adjusted), based on the percentage change reflected in the quarter ending December 31 of the two preceding years, minus 0.5%. The scheduled January 2000 adjustment of 3.4% was determined by taking the percentage increase in the Index between the fourth quarter ending December 31, 1997 and the fourth quarter ending December 31, 1998, which was 3.9%, and subtracting .5%.

## Vote Summary

- **07/15/99**—The House agreed (276-147, vote #300) to order the previous question on the rule (H.Res. 246) for consideration of H.R. 2490, the FY2000 Treasury and General Government Appropriations bill. H.Res. 246 was an open rule that allowed any germane amendment; an amendment to prohibit the pay adjustment, however, would not have been germane. By agreeing to order the previous question, Members voted not to consider an amendment to permit a pay raise prohibition amendment to be offered. Had the House not agreed to order the previous question, Members could have offered an amendment to the rule related to the pay adjustment. Under the terms of H.Res. 246, as adopted, an amendment seeking to halt the pay raise was not in order. The vote to order the previous question (and not allow any amendment to the rule) was seen by some as a vote to accept a pay adjustment.

## Proposed Reduction in Member Pay Adjustment

On October 28, 1999, the House rejected a motion to recommit the conference report on an appropriations bill, H.R. 3064, to instruct House managers to disagree with language in the report reducing the scheduled 3.4% January 2000 Member pay adjustment by 0.97%. The conference report on H.R. 3064, the FY2000 District of Columbia, Departments of Labor, Health and Human Services, and Education Appropriations bill, also provided in separate language a government-wide across-the-board rescission of 0.97% in discretionary budget authority for FY2000. Although the House and Senate agreed to the conference report with the pay and discretionary budget authority reduction provisions, H.R. 3064 was vetoed by the President on November 3, 1999.

- **10/28/99**—The House rejected (11-417, vote #548) a motion to recommit the conference report on H.R. 3064, District of Columbia, Departments of Labor, Health and Human Services, and Education Appropriations bill, FY2000, with instructions to House managers to disagree with pay language. Conference report pay language reduced the scheduled 3.4% January 2000 Member pay adjustment by 0.97% (H.Rept. 106-419, October 27, 1999, Division C (Rescissions and Offsets), §1001(e)).

- **10/28/99**—The House agreed (218-211, vote #549) to the conference report on H.R. 3064, which included language reducing the scheduled 3.4% January 2000 Member pay adjustment by 0.97%. H.R. 3064 was vetoed by the President on November 3, 1999.

# 1999

Members did not receive the scheduled January 1, 1999, 3.1% pay adjustment. The salary for Senators and Representatives remained $136,700.[61]

---

[61] The annual pay adjustment was determined by a formula based on the Employment Cost Index (the private industry, wages and salaries component), based on the percentage change reflected in the quarter ending December 31 for the two years prior, minus .5%. The scheduled January 1999 adjustment was determined by taking the percentage increase in the Index between the quarters October-December 1996 and October-December 1997, which was 3.9%, and subtracting .5%, giving a 3.4% increase. However, by law, Members may not receive an annual adjustment which is a (continued...)

## Actions on Annual Adjustment Scheduled for 1999

The conference version of H.R. 4104, the FY1999 Treasury, Postal Service, and General Government Appropriations bill, with a pay increase prohibition, was incorporated in the FY1999 Omnibus Consolidated and Emergency Supplemental Appropriations Act (H.R. 4328, P.L. 105-277).

## Vote Summary

- **07/15/98**—The House agreed (218-201, vote #284) to H.Res. 498, the rule providing for consideration of H.R. 4104. The rule waived points of order against language prohibiting a 1999 annual adjustment (§628 of the bill) for failure to comply with Rule XXI, Clause 2. The clause prohibits language in an appropriation bill that changes existing law. The effect of the rule was to ensure that the pay prohibition would not be procedurally challenged on the floor during debate on H.R. 4104. This did not preclude an amendment from being offered on the floor to challenge the prohibition.

- **07/16/98**—The House rejected (79-342, vote #289) an amendment that sought to strike Section 628 of H.R. 4104, which prohibited the January 1999 annual pay adjustment.

- **07/16/98**—The House passed (218-203, vote #293) H.R. 4104 with the pay prohibition language.

- **07/28/98**—The Senate adopted (voice vote) an amendment to S. 2312, the Senate version of the FY1999 Treasury Bill, which made the pay prohibition language in S. 2312 the same wording as the pay prohibition language in H.R. 4104. S. 2312, as reported (S.Rept. 105-251), contained language prohibiting the January 1999 pay adjustment.

- **09/03/98**—The Senate passed (91-5, vote #260) H.R. 4104, amended, in lieu of S. 2312, with the pay prohibition language.

- **10/01/98**—The House failed to agree (106-294, vote #476) to H.Res. 563, the rule waiving points of order against consideration of the conference report on H.R. 4104 (H.Rept. 105-592). As a result, the report was recommitted to conference. The pay prohibition language was not discussed during consideration of the rule.

- **10/07/98**—The House agreed (290-137, vote #494) to the conference report on H.R. 4104, with the pay prohibition language (H.Rept. 105-790). The Senate failed to reach agreement on adoption of the report. Conference report language was incorporated in H.R. 4328, the FY1999 Omnibus Consolidated and Emergency Supplemental Appropriations bill.

---

(...continued)

greater percentage increase than the percentage increase of the *base* pay of GS employees (P.L. 103-356, 108 Stat. 3410, October 13, 1994). Base pay is the pay rate before locality pay is added. Since General Schedule employees were limited to a 3.1% *base* pay increase in January 1999, Members were limited to 3.1%.

- **10/20/98**—The House agreed (333-95, vote #538) to the conference report accompanying H.R. 4328, the FY1999 Omnibus Consolidated and Emergency Supplemental Appropriations bill, with the pay prohibition language.

- **10/21/98**—The Senate agreed (65-29, vote #314) to the conference report accompanying H.R. 4328, with the pay prohibition. H.R. 4328 was signed into P.L. 105-277, on October 21, 1998.

# 1998

Members received the scheduled January 1, 1998, annual pay adjustment of 2.3%, increasing their salary from $133,600 to $136,700.[62]

## *Actions on Annual Adjustment Scheduled for 1998*

On July 17, 1997, the Senate adopted an amendment to prohibit the scheduled adjustment. The amendment was offered to S. 1023, the FY1998 Treasury and General Government Appropriations bill. The amendment did not apply to other top-level federal officials.

The House version of the Treasury bill was silent on the issue. The House version, H.R. 2378, was passed on September 17, 1997. Later that day, the Senate amended H.R. 2378 to include the language of its version in the nature of a substitute and passed the bill. The bill, with the pay prohibition, was then sent to the House.

On September 24, 1997, the House disagreed with the Senate substitute amendment and agreed to a conference. After lengthy discussion on the merits of a Member pay adjustment, the House voted to order the previous question on a pending motion to instruct conferees on an issue unrelated to the pay issue. Because the House permits only one motion to instruct conferees, and ordering the previous question precludes amendment to the pending question, this vote in effect foreclosed the possibility of instructing conferees to omit the pay adjustment from the conference report.

As a result of this House vote, H.R. 2378 was sent to conference by the House without instructions to prohibit the pay adjustment. Subsequently, the Senate language denying the increase was dropped in conference, and H.R. 2378 was signed into P.L. 105-61 on October 10, 1997, without the pay prohibition language.

## *Vote Summary*

- **07/17/97**—The Senate adopted (voice vote) an amendment prohibiting the scheduled January 1, 1998, annual adjustment for Members of Congress. The

---

[62] The pay adjustment was determined by a formula using the Employment Cost Index (private industry wages and salaries, not seasonally adjusted), based on the percentage change reflected in the quarter ending December 31 of the two preceding years, minus .5%. The scheduled adjustment of 2.9% was determined by taking the percentage increase in the Index between the quarters October-December 1995 and October-December 1996 which was 3.4% and subtracting .5%. However, Members were scheduled to receive a lesser adjustment of 2.3% because by law they may not receive an annual adjustment which is a greater percentage increase than the percentage increase of the base pay of GS employees. The base pay increase for the GS was limited to 2.3% by the President in August 1997.

amendment was offered to S. 1023, the FY1998 Treasury and General Government Appropriations bill.

- **07/22/97**—The Senate passed (99-0, vote 191) S. 1023 with the provision prohibiting the annual adjustment for Members of Congress.

- **09/17/97**—The Senate passed (voice vote) the House version of the FY1998 Treasury bill, H.R. 2378, after striking all after the enacting clause and substituting the language of S. 1023 as amended to include the pay prohibition.

- **09/24/97**—The House voted (229-199, vote 435) to order the previous question on a pending motion to instruct conferees on an issue unrelated to the pay issue. Because the House permits only one motion to instruct conferees, and because ordering the previous question precludes amendment to the pending question, this vote in effect foreclosed the possibility of instructing conferees to omit the pay adjustment from the conference report. As a result of this House vote, H.R. 2378 was sent to conference by the House without instructions to prohibit the pay adjustment. Conferees dropped the Senate pay amendment and both Houses agreed to the conference report on September 24, 1997. H.R. 2378 was signed into P.L. 105-61 on October 10, 1997.

## 1997

Members did not receive the annual pay adjustment of 2.3% scheduled for January 1, 1997, as a consequence of the votes taken in 1996. The salary of Members remained $133,600.

### *Actions on Annual Adjustment Scheduled for 1997*

The conference version of H.R. 3756 (the FY1997 Treasury and General Government Appropriations bill), with a pay adjustment prohibition, was incorporated into the FY1997 Omnibus Continuing Appropriations Act (H.R. 3610, P.L. 104-208).

### *Vote Summary*

- **07/16/96**—The House agreed (352-67, vote #317) to a floor amendment to H.R. 3756 prohibiting the 2.3% Member pay increase scheduled to take effect January 1, 1997. H.R. 3756 was the FY1997 Treasury and General Government Appropriations bill.

- **07/17/96**—The House passed (215-207, vote #323) H.R. 3756 with the provision prohibiting the annual adjustment for Members.

- **09/10/96**—After H.R. 3756 was reported by the Senate Committee on Appropriations, with amendments (S.Rept. 104-330), and without the House-passed pay prohibition provision, the Senate agreed by voice vote to a floor amendment (S.Amdt. 5208) prohibiting the annual pay adjustment. By unanimous consent, the Senate placed H.R. 3756 back on the calendar on September 12, 1996.

- **09/28/96**—The House agreed (370-37, vote #455) to the conference report on H.R. 3610, the Omnibus Continuing Appropriations bill, FY1997, which contained a pay freeze provision.

- **09/30/96**—The Senate agreed (voice vote) to the conference on H.R. 3610, the Omnibus Continuing Appropriations bill, FY1997, which contained a pay freeze provision. H.R. 3610 was enacted (P.L. 104-208), on September 30, 1996.

# 1996

Members did not receive the scheduled January 1, 1996, annual 2.3% adjustment as a consequence of the votes taken in 1995. The salary of Members remained $133,600.

## *Actions on Annual Adjustment Scheduled for 1996*

P.L. 104-52, the FY1996 Treasury and General Government Appropriations Act, included language prohibiting the adjustment.

## *Vote Summary*

- **08/05/95**—The Senate agreed (voice vote) to an amendment to H.R. 2020 prohibiting the Member pay adjustment of 2.3% scheduled to take effect in January 1996. The amendment did not apply to other top-level federal officials scheduled to receive the same 2.3% adjustment in January 1996.

- **08/05/95**—The Senate passed (voice vote) H.R. 2020 with the pay prohibition provision agreed to earlier in the day.

- **09/08/95**—The House approved (387-31, vote #648) a motion to instruct House conferees on H.R. 2020 to agree to the Senate amendment prohibiting the annual 2.3% adjustment scheduled in January 1996 for Members. The House disagreed to other Senate amendments and agreed to a conference.

- **11/15/95**—The House agreed (374-52, vote #797) to the conference on H.R. 2020 with a prohibition of the scheduled January 1996 pay increase.

- **11/15/95**—The Senate agreed (63-35, vote #576) to the conference on H.R. 2020 with a prohibition of the scheduled January 1996 Member pay increase. H.R. 2020 was signed into P.L. 104-52 on November 19, 1995.

# 1995

Members did not receive the scheduled January 1, 1995, annual 2.6% adjustment as a consequence of the votes taken in 1994. The salary of Members remained $133,600.

## *Actions on Annual Adjustment Scheduled for 1995*

P.L. 103-329, the FY1995 Treasury and General Government Appropriations Act, included language prohibiting the adjustment.

## *Vote Summary*

- **06/15/94**—The House passed (276-139, vote #247) H.R. 4539 with a provision denying the scheduled January 1, 1995, 2.6% annual adjustment. The pay provision had been included in the bill reported by the House Appropriations Committee (H.Rept. 103-534).

- **09/27/94**—The House agreed (360-53, vote #441) to the conference report on H.R. 4539 with the provision denying the annual adjustment.

- **09/28/94**—The Senate agreed (voice vote) to the conference report on H.R. 4539 with the provision denying the annual adjustment. H.R. 4539 was signed into law (P.L. 103-329) on September 30, 1994.

## Pay Freeze Proposal

During consideration of the budget resolution, a seven-year pay freeze was proposed but not adopted.

- **05/25/95**—The Senate passed a substitute amendment for the House-passed version of the FY1996 budget resolution (H.Con.Res. 67, 57-42, vote #232). The Senate version of the resolution (S.Con.Res. 13), which was reported on May 15, 1995, and considered in the Senate from May 19 until May 25, assumed a freeze on Member pay at $133,600 for seven years (S.Rept. 104-82). The conference agreement (H.Rept. 104-159) did not contain this language.

## Pay of Members of Congress During a Federal Government Shutdown

Legislation to prevent Member pay during a federal shutdown was considered but not enacted.

- **09/22/95**—The Senate adopted (voice vote) an amendment to the Senate version of the District of Columbia appropriations bill, FY1996 (S. 1244) providing that Members not be paid during a government shutdown, nor receive retroactive pay. The provision was also included in the Senate substitute amendment to H.R. 2546, the House version of the District of Columbia appropriations bill, on November 2, 1995. The provision was deleted in the conference report from January 31, 1996 (H.Rept. 104-455). Members were paid during the November 14-19, 1995, and December 16, 1995 - January 5, 1996, shutdowns because their pay is automatically funded in a permanent appropriation.

- **10/27/1995**—The Senate accepted an amendment (S.Amdt. 3013) to S. 1357, the Balanced Budget Reconciliation Act of 1995. This amendment would prohibit pay for Members of Congress and the President during a lapse in appropriations.

- **11/28/1995**—The Senate accepted an amendment (S.Amdt. 3065) to S. 1396, the Interstate Commerce Commission Sunset Act of 1995. The language was included in the Senate amendment to H.R. 2539, the House version of this bill, but not in the conference report.

- Numerous measures were introduced during the 104th Congress to prevent pay for Members of Congress in the event of a shutdown (H.R. 2281, H.R. 2639, H.R. 2658, H.R. 2671, H.R. 2373, H.R. 2855, H.R. 2828, H.R. 2882, S. 1220, S. 1428, S. 1480, and H.Con.Res. 113). These bills were referred to committee, but no further action was taken.

## 1994

Members did not receive the scheduled January 1, 1994, 2.1% adjustment as a consequence of votes taken in 1993 to prohibit the annual adjustment. The salary of Members remained $133,600.

### *Actions on Annual Adjustment Scheduled for 1994*

Votes to prohibit the scheduled January 1, 1994, annual adjustment were taken during consideration of the Senate Committee Funding Resolution (S.Res. 71) and the Unemployment Compensation Act (S. 382, H.R. 920).

### *Vote Summary*

- **02/24/93**—The Senate adopted (voice vote) an amendment to the Senate Committee Funding Resolution (S.Res. 71) expressing the sense of the Senate that Senators' pay be frozen for eleven months in calendar year 1994. This non-binding language in effect denied the scheduled 2.1% January 1994 annual pay adjustment for Senators.

- **02/24/93**—The Senate adopted (98-0, vote #16) an amendment to the previous amendment (see above) changing the pay freeze period to one year.

- **02/25/93**—The Senate agreed (94-2, vote #20) to S.Res. 71 with the non-binding amendment freezing Senators' pay for one year in calendar year 1994.

- **03/03/93**—The Senate adopted (voice vote) an amendment to S. 382, the Emergency Unemployment Compensation Act, denying the scheduled 2.1% adjustment for Members on January 1, 1994.

- **03/03/93**—The Senate agreed (58-41, vote #23) to a motion to table an amendment to S. 382 prohibiting adjustments for *all* federal employees.

- **03/03/93**—The Senate passed (66-33, vote #24) H.R. 920, the House version of the Emergency Unemployment Compensation Act, with a provision denying the scheduled 2.1% adjustment for Members on January 1, 1994.[63]

- **03/04/93**—The House agreed (403-0, vote #54) to a motion to agree to the Senate pay amendment to H.R. 920. H.R. 920 was signed into law (P.L. 103-6, 107 Stat. 35, March 4, 1993, §7).

### *Pay Reduction Proposal*

The Senate considered two pay-related amendments to S. 1935, the Congressional Gifts Reform bill. The bill passed the Senate, but no further action was taken.

- **05/05/94**—The Senate rejected an amendment (S.Amdt. 1680) to S. 1935 requiring Member pay to be reduced immediately by 15% (34-59, vote #103).

---

[63] Before passage, the Senate substituted the language of S. 382, as amended.

- **05/06/94**—An amendment (S.Amdt. 1682) stating, "It is the sense of the Senate that any Member who voted May 5, 1994, to amend S. 1935 to reduce the pay of Members of the Senate by 15 percent should return to the U.S. Treasury the full amount of any pay that would not have been received had the amendment been enacted into law and that such Members should provide evidence to the public on an annual basis that they have done so," was withdrawn.

## 1993

On January 1, 1993, Members received an annual adjustment of 3.2%, increasing pay from $129,500 to $133,600. No votes were held in 1992 to prohibit the adjustment.

## 1992

Pursuant to the Ethics Reform Act of 1989, Representatives and Senators received an annual adjustment of 3.5% on January 1, 1992, increasing their pay from $125,100 to $129,500. No votes were held in 1991 to deny the scheduled adjustment.

### *Recognition of Ratification of 27ᵗʰ Amendment to the Constitution*

The House and Senate both recognized ratification of the 27ᵗʰ Amendment to the Constitution, which provides that a pay adjustment for Members of Congress shall not take effect until an intervening election has occurred.[64]

- **05/20/92**—The House adopted (414-3, vote #131) H.Con.Res. 320, recognizing ratification of the 27ᵗʰ Amendment.

- **05/20/92**—The Senate adopted S.Con.Res. 120 (99-0, vote #99), recognizing adoption of the Amendment and S.Res. 298 (99-0, vote #100), also recognizing the Amendment's adoption.

## 1991

Representatives and Senators received a 3.6% pay increase in January 1991 pursuant to the annual adjustment procedure established in Section 704 of the Ethics Reform Act (P.L. 101-194). Pursuant to Section 703 of the Ethics Reform Act, Representatives' pay was also adjusted by 25%. Representatives' pay increased from $96,600 to $125,100,[65] and Senators' pay increased from $98,400 to $101,900.

---

[64] The amendment had been certified officially on May 18, 1992, by the U.S. Archivist and published in the *Federal Register* on May 19, 1992. The pay amendment was among five amendments proposed to the United States Constitution and submitted to the States along with the Bill of Rights on September 25, 1789. These proposed amendments did not contain ratification deadlines. The five amendments had failed to be approved by the necessary three-fourths of the States as provided by Article V of the Constitution, until the pay amendment was finally ratified in 1992.

[65] Upon receipt of the salary increase, Representatives were prohibited from accepting honoraria and were limited to 15% of salary in other forms of outside earned income, effective January 1, 1991. Although not providing Senators with an increase comparable to the 25% increase for Representatives, the Ethics Reform Act decreased permissible 1990 honoraria received by Senators from the 1989 limit of 40% to 27% of salary. Further, the act stipulated that future (continued...)

---

Subsequently, the Senate voted to increase its pay by 22.8% to equal the salary of Representatives (from $101,900 to $125,100), in the Legislative Branch Appropriations bill, FY1992 (H.R. 2506). The House agreed to this action.

## Vote Summary

- **07/17/91**—The Senate adopted (53-45, vote #133) an amendment to H.R. 2506 increasing Senators' pay to equal Representatives' pay; banning honoraria for Senators; and limiting their outside earned income to 15% of salary.

- **07/17/91**—The Senate passed (voice vote) H.R. 2506 with the pay provision.

- **07/31/91**—The House agreed (voice vote) to the conference report on H.R. 2506 with Senate pay provision.

- **08/02/91**—The Senate agreed (voice vote) to the conference report on H.R. 2506 with the pay provision. H.R. 2506 was signed into law (P.L. 102-90) August 14, 1991. The pay increase became effective the same day.

# 1990

Section 702 of the Ethics Reform Act of 1989 (P.L. 101-194) restored the previously denied January 1989 and 1990 annual adjustments (4.1% and 3.6%), compounded, for Representatives. Representatives' pay was increased 7.9%, from $89,500 to $96,600, effective February 1, 1990.

Section 1101 of the Ethics Reform Act also adjusted Senators' pay. Effective February 1, 1990, pay was increased by 9.9%, from $89,500 to $98,400. This increase represented restoration of the previously denied 1988, 1989, and 1990 adjustments (2.0%, 4.1%, and 3.6%), compounded.

Later in 1990, the Senate voted to reduce Member pay in an amendment to S. 110, the Family Planning Amendments bill, although a cloture motion subsequently failed.

## Vote Summary

- **09/26/90**—The Senate adopted (S.Amdt. 2884, 96-1, vote #254) a Member pay amendment to the substitute amendment reported by the Committee on Labor and Human Resources to S. 110. The amendment would have reduced Member salary by an amount corresponding to the percentage reduction of pay of federal employees who were furloughed or otherwise had their pay reduced resulting from a sequestration order.[66]

- **09/26/90**—The Senate rejected (50-46, vote #256) a motion to invoke cloture on the Committee on Labor and Human Resources substitute amendment, which

---

(...continued)

Senate pay raises be accompanied by a dollar-for-dollar decrease in permissible honoraria until the honoraria limit was less than or equal to 1% of a Senator's salary, which would then result in prohibiting the acceptance of honoraria.

[66] A sequestration order is a cancellation of part of a federal agency's budget, thereby reducing funds available for expenditure by an agency. Sequestration is determined by the Office of Management and Budget under the Budget Enforcement Act of 1990 and the Omnibus Budget Reconciliation Act of 1993.

contained the Member pay provision. Subsequently, S. 110 was pulled from further consideration on the Senate floor by its sponsor.

## Author Contact Information

Ida A. Brudnick
Specialist on the Congress
ibrudnick@crs.loc.gov, 7-6460

## Acknowledgments

A previous version of this report was written by Paul E. Dwyer, formerly a Specialist in American National Government at CRS, who has since retired.